★ THE CIVIL WAR THROUGH PRIMARY SOURCES ★

An Overview of the American Civil War through Primary Sources

Carin T. Ford

Enslow Publishers, Inc.
40 Industrial Road
Box 398
Berkeley Heights, NJ 07922
USA

http://www.enslow.com

Copyright © 2013 by Enslow Publishers, Inc.

All rights reserved.

No part of this book may be reproduced by any means without the written permission of the publisher.

Original edition published as *The American Civil War: An Overview* in 2004.

Library of Congress Cataloging-in-Publication Data

Ford, Carin T.
 [American Civil War]
 An overview of the American Civil War through primary sources / Carin T. Ford.
    p. cm. — (The Civil War through primary sources)
 Originally published: The American Civil War. Berkeley Heights, NJ : Enslow Publishers, c2004.
 Summary: "Introduces the American Civil War, including the causes of the conflict, background on the Union and the Confederacy, the major battles and important historical figures, and how the Union won the war"— Provided by publisher.
 Includes bibliographical references and index.
 ISBN 978-0-7660-4124-0
 1. United States—History—Civil War, 1861–1865—Juvenile literature. I. Title.
 E468.F717 2014
 973.7—dc23
                    2012030113

Future editions:
Paperback ISBN: 978-1-4644-0182-4
EPUB ISBN: 978-1-4645-1095-3
Single-User PDF ISBN: 978-1-4646-1095-0
Multi-User PDF ISBN: 978-0-7660-5724-1

Printed in China

012013 Leo Paper Group, Heshan City, Guangdong, China

10 9 8 7 6 5 4 3 2 1

To Our Readers: We have done our best to make sure all Internet addresses in this book were active and appropriate when we went to press. However, the author and the publisher have no control over and assume no liability for the material available on those Internet sites or on other Web sites they may link to. Any comments or suggestions can be sent by e-mail to comments@enslow.com or to the address on the back cover.

Illustration Credits: Enslow Publishers, Inc., p. 10; Library of Congress Prints and Photographs, pp. 1, 2–3, 4, 5, 7, 8, 12, 13, 16, 18, 20, 22, 24, 26, 29, 30, 32, 35, 36, 37, 39; U.S. National Park Service, p. 40.

Cover Illustration: Library of Congress Prints and Photographs (Illustration of the Battle of Atlanta).

CONTENTS

1. **NORTH AGAINST SOUTH** 5
2. **THE WAR BEGINS** 13
3. **MANY MORE BATTLES** 20
4. **THE TIDE TURNS** 29
5. **PEACE AT LAST?** 36

    Timeline 42

    Chapter Notes 44

    Glossary 46

    Further Reading
      (Books and Internet Addresses) 47

    Index 48

LOOK FOR THIS SYMBOL PRIMARY SOURCE **TO FIND THE PRIMARY SOURCES THROUGHOUT THIS BOOK.**

Primary Source

In this 1862 photograph, African-American slaves plant sweet potatoes at Hopkinson's Plantation in South Carolina. The issue of slavery stirred up a conflict in the United States in the mid-1800s.

CHAPTER 1

NORTH AGAINST SOUTH

The people of the United States faced a big question in the 1800s: What should be done about slavery?

The businesses, factories, and small farms of the North did not depend on slave labor. As time passed, most people in the Northern states had come to believe that slavery was wrong. One by one, these states had been putting an end to slavery.

On the large farms of the South, however, 4 million slaves were forced to work in the fields, growing cotton, rice, and tobacco. Slaves worked from sunrise to sunset. They were bought and sold like animals. They were given little food or clothing, and their masters often beat them.

An OVERVIEW of the AMERICAN CIVIL WAR Through PRIMARY SOURCES

Some Southerners believed slavery was wrong—yet they still thought it was needed. The South grew most of the cotton sold in the world. Without slaves, who would work in the fields? Southerners were afraid they would lose a lot of money, as well as their way of life, if they did not have slaves to grow their cotton.

In addition, people in the South did not think the federal government had the right to tell them whether they could—or could not—have slaves. They believed it was up to the people of each state to decide for themselves.

Meanwhile, the United States was growing. New states and territories were becoming part of the country. Should slavery be allowed in these areas?

Questions about slavery were nothing new. As early as 1787, Thomas Jefferson, James Madison, and other important American leaders had talked about these problems when they were writing the U.S. Constitution. They were not sure whether they should write laws that would do away with slavery.

PRIMARY SOURCE

Slaves were often treated cruelly and punished harshly. This 1807 woodcut shows an iron mask, collar, leg shackles, and spurs used to restrict slaves. Northerners wanted to get rid of slavery, but Southerners said it was necessary for their economy to survive.

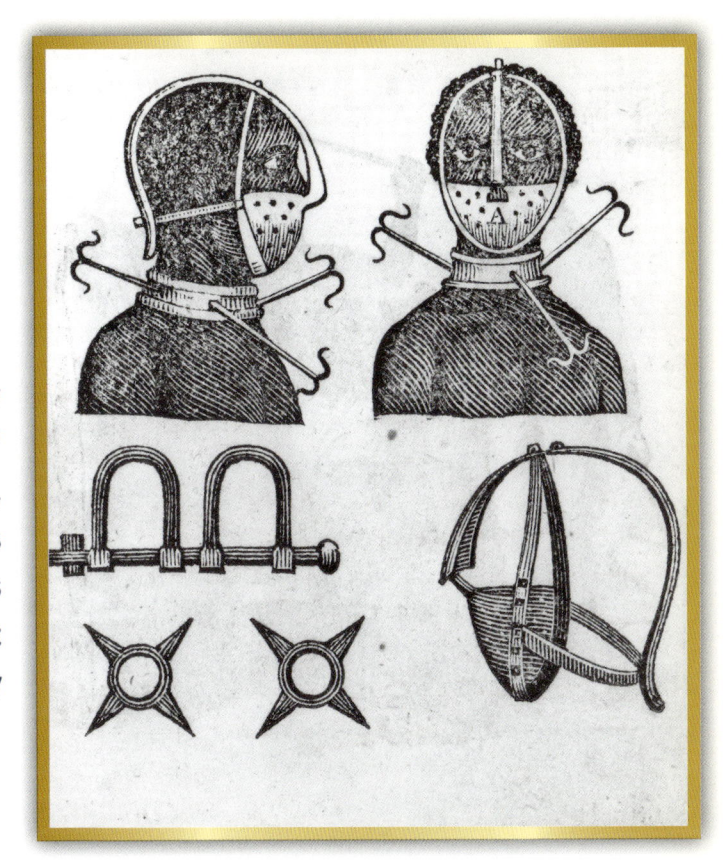

They finally decided it was not worth arguing about. They wanted to make sure that all the states joined the newly formed United States of America. If the Constitution outlawed slavery, Southerners might not want to be part of the new nation.

Besides, in the 1780s, it had seemed as if slavery was on its way out. Many Northern states had already taken steps to get rid of it. In the South, farmers grew less tobacco, so fewer slaves were needed.

An OVERVIEW of the AMERICAN CIVIL WAR Through PRIMARY SOURCES

Then, in 1793, Eli Whitney invented the cotton gin. With this new machine to pick out the seeds, cleaning cotton was faster and more efficient. As long as plantation owners had hundreds of men and women to work in the fields, they could grow and sell tons of cotton.

The issue of slavery was tied up with the issue of states' rights. Many Southerners did not like the federal government telling them what to do. In 1832, South Carolina had talked about breaking away from the country when the government passed a tax law the state did not want to obey.

Primary Source

President Abraham Lincoln often spoke out against slavery.

Bleeding Kansas

There was fighting over slavery even before the Civil War broke out. When Kansas was made a territory in 1854, the people there had to decide whether it would be a slave state or a free state. Fighting between the two sides was so horrible—and went on so long—the area was called "Bleeding Kansas." It entered the Union as a free state in January 1861.

The problem of slavery never went away. In fact, it got worse through the years. By the mid-1800s, it looked as if the country might split in half over slavery.

Abraham Lincoln was elected president in 1860. He often spoke out against slavery. "If slavery is not wrong, nothing is wrong," he said.[1] Yet Lincoln also knew that there was a great deal of tension between the North and South. He worried that if he tried to get rid of slavery, Southerners might secede, or break away, from the United States and form their own country. Lincoln did not want the United States torn in half. So he did not talk about ending slavery. Instead, he argued that slavery should not be allowed to spread into new areas.

An OVERVIEW of the AMERICAN CIVIL WAR
Through PRIMARY SOURCES

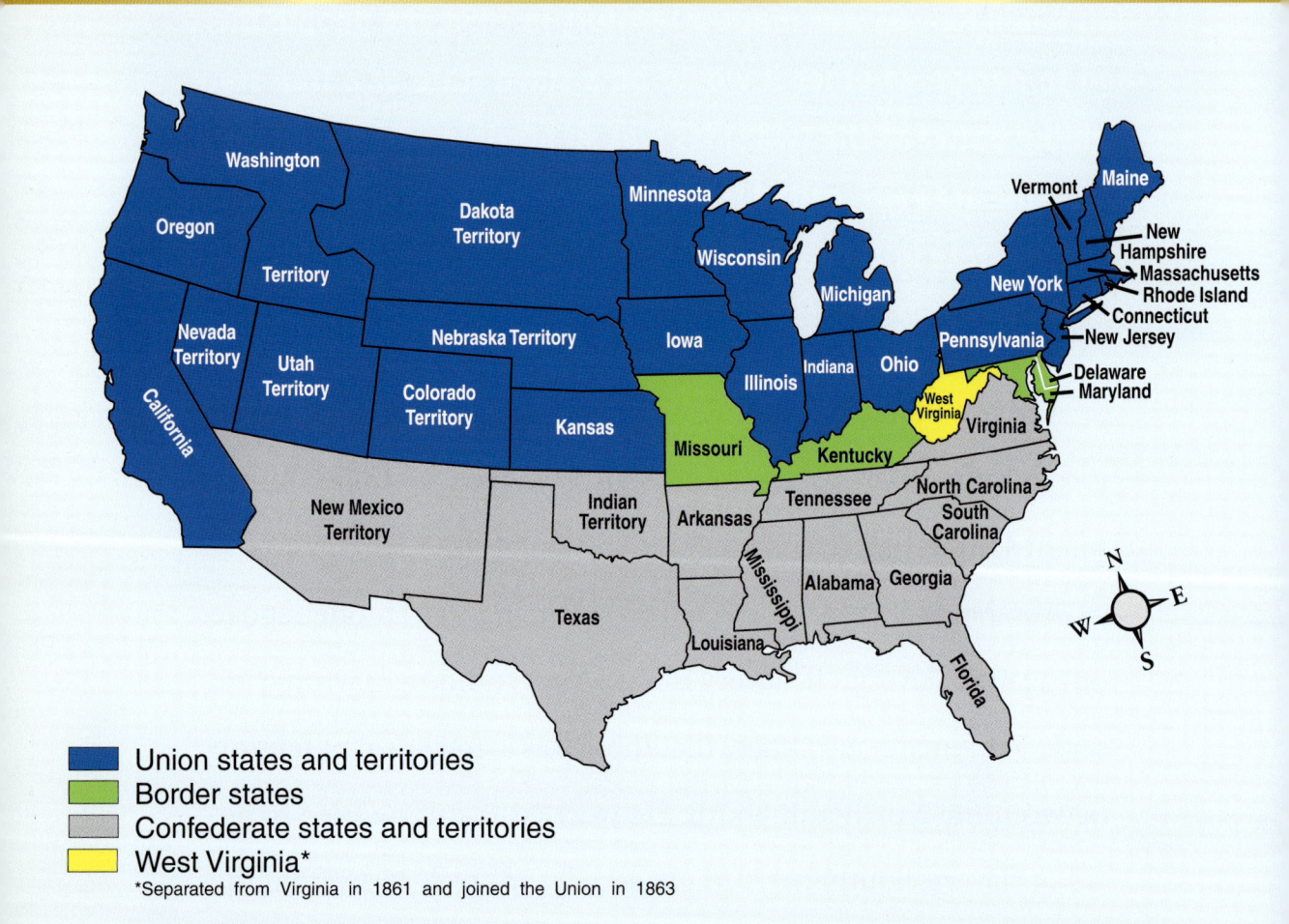

- **Union states and territories**
- **Border states**
- **Confederate states and territories**
- **West Virginia***

*Separated from Virginia in 1861 and joined the Union in 1863

In December 1860, South Carolina seceded from the Union. Soon, other Southern states left, too. This map shows the United States divided between Union and Confederacy during the Civil War.

North Against South

Still, the people in the South worried that Lincoln would try to put an end to slavery everywhere. In December 1860, South Carolina seceded from the United States. Alabama, Florida, Mississippi, Louisiana, Texas, and Georgia soon followed.

They formed their own country, the Confederate States of America, and Jefferson Davis was elected their president. "We feel that our cause is just and holy," he said.[2]

Most Southerners reacted joyfully to the news. "We have a country at last, to live for, to pray for, and, if need be, to die for!" said Lucius Quintus Lamar, a former Mississippi congressman.[3]

Yet not everyone thought the decision to secede was wise. "You people of the South don't know what you are doing," said William Tecumseh Sherman. "This country will be drenched in blood. . . . You are rushing into war . . . [and] are bound to fail."[4]

Sherman went on to become a famous general for the North during the Civil War—and his words came true. During the next four years, more than 600,000 men would give their lives in the bloodiest war ever fought on American soil.

Primary Source

This photo shows the interior of Fort Sumter with the Confederate flag flying after the South's victory over the Union. This battle marked the first combat of the Civil War.

CHAPTER 2

THE WAR BEGINS

The new Confederate government soon began taking over all the U.S. forts and arsenals—where weapons are stored—in the South. President Lincoln did not want war. More than anything else, he wanted to put the country back together peacefully. "There will be no blood shed unless it be forced upon the Government," Lincoln said in February 1861.[1]

Fort Sumter sat on an island in South Carolina's Charleston Harbor. Soldiers from South Carolina had taken over the nearby forts. They wanted to control Fort Sumter, too.

An OVERVIEW of the AMERICAN CIVIL WAR
Through PRIMARY SOURCES

The fort was under the command of Union major Robert Anderson. He and his sixty-eight men were running out of food and water. They could hold out only a few more weeks.

Lincoln decided to send a ship to the fort with supplies. He said he would not send guns or extra soldiers, as long as the fort and the ship were not attacked.

Lincoln had made up his mind . . . and so had Jefferson Davis. Before sunrise on April 12, four men from the Confederacy rowed to Fort Sumter with a message: If the Union troops did not give up the fort within an hour, the Confederates would open fire.

Anderson would not surrender. At 4:30 A.M., the Confederates fired a cannon. Fort Sumter was under attack. Shells battered the fort for a day and a half while crowds of onlookers cheered from their rooftops in Charleston. Anderson had little ammunition, few men . . . and no hope of winning. He was forced to surrender.

The Civil War had begun.

Soon after the attack, four more states joined the Confederacy: Virginia, Arkansas, Tennessee, and North Carolina. Lincoln called

The War Begins

for 75,000 men to volunteer in the Union army. They were asked to serve for only three months. No one in the North or South thought the war would last long.

Four days later, Lincoln declared a blockade of all Southern ports. The Union navy was not going to let any ships in or out of

Who Would Win the Civil War?

WHY THE NORTH EXPECTED TO WIN

- ★ The North had more men to fight: The 7 million white people who lived in the South were up against about 22 million people in the North.
- ★ There were more factories in the North to make guns and bullets.
- ★ The North had more railroads for carrying men and supplies from place to place.

WHY THE SOUTH EXPECTED TO WIN

- ★ Northerners did not know their way around the South, where the fighting would take place.
- ★ Southern farmers were already very skilled at shooting guns and riding horses. That gave them an advantage.
- ★ Southerners were fighting to save their way of life, so winning was very important to them.

Confederate soldiers drove the Union troops from the battlefield at the First Battle of Bull Run in Manassas, Virginia. After the battle, some Confederate soldiers went home because they thought the war was over. But it was only just beginning.

the South. This would be a major problem for the Southern states. They needed to sell their cotton in England and other European countries. In addition, the blockade would stop ships that were coming in to deliver food or supplies to the South.

Three months after the battle at Fort Sumter, a volunteer Union army headed south for Virginia. The men were led by General Irvin McDowell. The Confederate army, under General Pierre Beauregard, waited by Bull Run Creek near Manassas, Virginia.

The War Begins

Many people from Washington, D.C., came out on that hot summer's day, July 21, to watch the fighting. They arrived in carriages and brought picnic baskets and binoculars. They thought the Union army would win quickly and easily.

As shots rang out during the afternoon, the Union seemed to be winning. But when more Confederate soldiers arrived, it was too much for the Union. The Northerners had already gone for half a day without any food or water. They were hot, tired, and thirsty.

The Union soldiers withdrew from the battlefield, pushing and shoving. "Turn back! Turn back! We are whipped!" the soldiers cried as they ran.[2] In panic, they headed back to Washington, D.C.

The Blue & The Gray

The Union uniform was blue, and the Confederate uniform was gray. But clothing was scarce during the war, especially in the South. It was common for soldiers to wear the enemy's "colors" and mistakenly fire on their own men during battle.

PRIMARY SOURCE

Soldiers on both sides of the fight were in for a long war. In the left-hand portrait, a young unidentified Confederate soldier holds an artillery saber. In the right-hand photo, an unidentified Union soldier holds his bayoneted musket.

The War Begins

The Confederates did not chase after them. They were overjoyed, believing they had won not just the battle but the war. Some Southern soldiers thought the war was over, so they went home. However, they were wrong.

During the war, the Confederates were known for giving a "rebel yell" during battle. It began at Bull Run, when General Thomas J. "Stonewall" Jackson told his men to "yell like furies." Most of the soldiers were fox hunters who made "yip-yip" yells to call their hunting dogs. That is what the rebel yell sounded like.[3]

The North and the South gave different names to the same Civil War battles. The South used the names of nearby towns, such as Manassas. The North used landmarks, such as Bull Run, a local stream. What the South called the "Battle of Manassas" was known in the North as the "Battle of Bull Run."

Bull Run was only the first of many battles. The fighting was far from over. Lincoln called up 100,000 more soldiers. They would serve for three years, not three months. It was now clear: This would not be a short war.

CHAPTER 3

MANY MORE BATTLES

General George B. McClellan took charge of the Union troops after the first Battle of Bull Run. He was an organized man. He drilled his soldiers for eight hours a day and turned them into a well-trained army.

McClellan's problem, however, was that he never felt ready to fight. He was slow to move, always asking for more men and more time.

He finally marched his troops to Virginia in October 1861. There, he lost a battle at Ball's Bluff. President Lincoln hoped that at some point, McClellan would attack Richmond, Virginia,

Many More Battles

the capital of the Confederacy. The president also wanted some military action in the West, mainly Kentucky, Tennessee, and Missouri.

Leading the Union army in the West was Ulysses S. Grant, a graduate of the U.S. Military Academy at West Point. Grant was a great general. He explained his idea of war: "Find out where your enemy is. Get at him as soon as you can. Strike him as hard as you can, and keep moving!"[1]

Fighting alongside the U.S. navy in February 1862, Grant led Union troops in the easy capture of Fort Henry in Tennessee. A week later, he took Fort Donelson, just twelve miles away.

After capturing Fort Donelson, Grant was asked to give his terms of surrender. He replied, "No terms except an unconditional and immediate surrender."[2] This meant that he demanded a total surrender. There would be no special deals. His answer became famous, and many people joked that "U.S. Grant" actually stood for "Unconditional Surrender Grant."

The Civil War featured the first-ever naval battle between ships covered in iron armor. The Union *Monitor* and the Confederate *Merrimack* battled to a draw.

After losing forts Henry and Donelson, Confederate general Albert S. Johnston withdrew into western Tennessee to reorganize his men. Many people thought of Johnston as one of the finest soldiers in the North or South.

Grant followed with his troops to Pittsburgh Landing, Tennessee, near Shiloh Church. There he waited for the arrival of more Union troops under General Don Carlos Buell. The armies planned to march together into Mississippi.

Many More Battles

Grant waited, never thinking the Confederates might try attacking his army first. But that is exactly what happened. While Grant's men spent the April day drilling, swimming, and resting, Johnston's men were marching toward them.

On April 6, Confederate soldiers surprised the Union men, and a bloody battle took place. Few men on either side had been in battle before. "Why, it's just like shooting squirrels," said one Illinois soldier, trying to stir the men to action, "only these squirrels have guns, that's all."[3]

A Battle of Iron Giants

In March 1862, the first-ever battle between two ships covered in iron armor took place.

The Confederate ship *Merrimack* and the Union *Monitor* were called the "ironclads." Cannonballs that would have sunk a wooden ship just bounced off the ironclads. In the battle of the *Merrimack* and the *Monitor*, neither of the ironclad ships was badly damaged. No winner was declared. Both navies decided that from then on, all ships would be ironclads.

PRIMARY SOURCE

Union general Ulysses S. Grant (left) poses for a portrait at his headquarters in Cold Harbor, Virginia, in 1864. Confederate general Robert E. Lee (right) stands for a portrait taken by famous photographer Mathew Brady sometime between 1864 and 1865.

Many More Battles

Hundreds of terrified soldiers on both sides ran and hid during the fighting. Private Luke Barber of the 15th Illinois Infantry recalled, "Our brave boys were dropping by scores. . . . Thick as hailstones the bullets whistled through my hair and around my cheek." Barber went to help an injured officer, then hurried back to join his company. He was shocked, he said, "to find not one living member of the 15th Regiment."[4]

Buell's army arrived with 25,000 soldiers that night to help Grant. The following day, the Confederates were forced to retreat. There were too many Union soldiers. Of the 100,000 men who fought in the two-day battle, nearly 25,000 were killed or wounded.

Some newspaper editors said the army should get rid of Grant because he had nearly lost the bloody battle at Shiloh. Lincoln replied, "I can't spare this man, he *fights*."[5] The president was not as happy with the slow-moving McClellan. Lincoln wrote to the general in late May, "I think the time is near when you must either attack Richmond or give up the job."[6]

The Battle of Antietam, depicted in this illustration, was the single bloodiest day of fighting during the war.

So, McClellan marched his men toward Richmond. The Confederate army was waiting for him, led by the brilliant general Robert E. Lee. Another graduate of West Point, Lee did not believe in slavery or secession. At the start of the war, he had been asked to lead the Union army. But Lee said he would not fight against his home state of Virginia.

Although McClellan had 100,000 well-trained soldiers, he could not defeat Lee's army. All this fighting near Richmond was called the Seven Days' Battles. In late August, a second Battle

Many More Battles

of Bull Run took place. There were more Union soldiers than Confederates. Yet once again, the Union army was driven from the field.

The Confederate army now pressed into Maryland. This was the first time General Lee tried to bring the war to the North. The Battle of Antietam, near Sharpsburg, Maryland, took place on September 17, 1862. Fighting lasted fourteen hours, and it was the single bloodiest day in the war—24,000 men were killed, wounded, or missing. When a Confederate officer was asked where his men were, he replied, "Dead on the field."[7]

Lee finally took his troops back across the Potomac River. McClellan did not follow the Confederate army. He allowed them to retreat to Virginia. This was the last straw for Lincoln. On November 5, 1862, he removed McClellan as head of the Union army.

The North claimed the victory at Antietam. It was more of a draw than a victory, but it was enough for Lincoln. He had been waiting for a chance to strike a blow against slavery. If the slaves

An OVERVIEW of the AMERICAN CIVIL WAR
Through PRIMARY SOURCES

were free, they would be able to join the Union army. Also, the cotton and tobacco fields in the South would be left without workers, and this would weaken the Confederacy. Lincoln said that freeing the slaves had become a "military necessity"—that is, he had to do it to win the war.[8]

A draft of the Emancipation Proclamation was published in September 1862. The document declared that all slaves in the rebelling states of the Confederacy would be "forever free."[9] The final proclamation was issued on January 1, 1863.

In truth, no slaves were freed right after the Emancipation Proclamation. Lincoln was not the president of the Confederacy, so Southerners did not obey his orders. Yet the Emancipation Proclamation was very important: It showed the world that the reason for the war had changed. It had started as a war to keep the country from splitting in two. Now the war was being fought to free the slaves.

CHAPTER 4

THE TIDE TURNS

Lincoln was growing restless. With all the factories, shipyards, guns, and men in the North, his army should have been winning battle after battle. Yet it was not. Lincoln needed a general who could win.

He made General Ambrose Burnside commander of the Union army. But General Burnside, too, would not last long. At the close of 1862, his army of 122,000 men lost to Lee's army of only 78,500 in a battle at Fredericksburg, Virginia. Lincoln then brought in General Joseph Hooker to replace General Burnside.

PRIMARY SOURCE

This photo shows a dead Confederate soldier after the Battle of Gettysburg. During the battle, General Robert E. Lee lost about 28,000 soldiers—one-third of his army.

Hooker, who was nicknamed "Fighting Joe," said he would destroy the Confederate army. But Hooker lost a battle at Chancellorsville, Virginia, in May 1863. The Union had twice as many men as the Confederates, yet the leadership of Confederate generals James E. B. "Jeb" Stuart and "Stonewall" Jackson forced the Union soldiers to retreat.

By the summer of 1863, Lee was ready to invade the North. His army had won so many battles in the past two years that Lee believed he could not be beaten. He also knew that most Northerners had grown tired of the war. If he could win a major victory on Union soil, maybe the North would call an end to the war.

The Tide Turns

Lee marched his 75,000 men up to central Pennsylvania in late June. He bumped into Union cavalry—soldiers on horseback—near the town of Gettysburg. Fighting broke out on July 1, 1863.

The fighting was fierce for two days. Thousands of soldiers were killed or wounded. Yet under the command of General George Meade, the Union army held its position. Meade was the fifth commander of the Union army in less than a year. Lincoln had just put him in charge, replacing Hooker.

On July 3, Lee made one last attempt to win the battle. He ordered 15,000 Confederate soldiers to march across an open field, straight at the center of the Union line. The Union troops waited behind a low wall until the Confederates came within range. Then they shot down row after row of soldiers.

A Massachusetts soldier recalled, "Wounded men who could no longer stand, struggled, fought, shouted and killed—hatless, coatless, drowned in sweat . . . red with blood."[1]

This illustration depicts Pickett's Charge. During this bold Confederate attack, 15,000 soldiers marched across the field toward the Union line. Row after row of Southern soldiers were gunned down.

The three-day Battle of Gettysburg was the bloodiest battle during the Civil War. Lee was forced to retreat. He had lost one-third of his army—close to 28,000 men.

The Union had also suffered a huge loss of 23,000 men. Yet the North was able to get more men, weapons, and ammunition. The South was running out of men as well as supplies. They also had very little food to eat. Sometimes they went for days eating nothing but dry corn.[2] The Battle of Gettysburg is called the turning point of the Civil War. The South never recovered its strength after this battle.

The Tide Turns

A Draft and Riots

The Union needed more soldiers. In March 1863, the government passed a law drafting men into the army. A man could avoid the draft by paying $300 to hire someone to take his place. Many people thought this was unfair. Riots broke out in cities, such as New York, and thousands were killed or wounded.

The Confederate loss at Gettysburg took place at the same time that Union general Grant's forces took Vicksburg, Mississippi. When Grant captured Port Hudson, Louisiana, several days later, the North gained total control of the Mississippi River. The Confederacy was now split in half.

In September 1863, a Confederate victory at Chickamauga, Georgia, gave Southerners hope that they still had a chance. Several months later, however, Lincoln put Grant in charge of the entire Union army. Grant would lead his troops in the East. General William Tecumseh Sherman would march through the South from the Mississippi River to the coast of Georgia.

An OVERVIEW of the AMERICAN CIVIL WAR Through PRIMARY SOURCES

The war would last another year, but it now seemed to be just a question of time before the Union won. Grant's army headed for Virginia. They wanted to capture Richmond, the capital of the Confederacy. On May 5, 1864, fighting began in a wooded area called the Wilderness.

It was a horrible struggle. Soldiers became lost in the woods and shot at their own men. The trees caught fire and hundreds of men burned to death. Both armies suffered terrible losses—close to 18,000 Union soldiers and nearly 7,800 Confederates. Lee could not replace the soldiers he had lost. The South was quickly running out of men who could fight.

Pickett's Charge

The march across the open field at Gettysburg became known as Pickett's Charge. When it was over, General Lee said, "It was all my fault."[3] Confederate general George Pickett never forgave Lee for the deaths of his men.

Primary Source

Union general William Tecumseh Sherman's troops move ammunition in wheelbarrows from Fort McAllister near Savannah, Georgia. Sherman led 100,000 soldiers on a march through Georgia, destroying everything in the army's path to cripple the Confederates.

Meanwhile, Sherman was marching from Tennessee toward Atlanta, Georgia, with 100,000 men. As he made his way through the South, Sherman destroyed everything in sight. He was a nervous man, who did not sleep much. He was also practical and focused on the task he had to do. Sherman's men burned buildings and tore up railroad tracks. They left behind a pathway forty miles wide in ruins.

"War is cruelty. . . . The crueler it is, the sooner it will be over," Sherman said.[4] His attack on Atlanta lasted from mid-July to September. Finally, on September 2, 1864, Sherman sent a message to Lincoln, "Atlanta is ours."[5] The people in the North breathed a sigh of relief. The war would soon end.

CHAPTER 5

PEACE AT LAST?

On November 8, 1864, Abraham Lincoln was elected to a second term as president. The next week, Sherman burned Atlanta to the ground. He then began his "march to the sea." Again, his soldiers destroyed everything as they went. He wanted the South to give up all hope of winning. "They say no living thing is found in Sherman's track," wrote a Southern woman.[1]

Sherman made his way to Savannah, Georgia, and captured that city on December 21. Next, he marched his men north through the Carolinas. He destroyed the railroads into Charleston, and the city fell in February. The United States flag that had

Peace at Last?

PRIMARY SOURCE

A political campaign button from Abraham Lincoln's second campaign for president of the United States. Lincoln was reelected on November 8, 1864. By that time, the war had turned greatly in the Union's favor.

been removed from Fort Sumter at the start of the war now flew again. "I thank God that I have lived to see this day," said Robert Anderson, who had surrendered Fort Sumter to the Confederates four years earlier.[2]

Lincoln was sworn into office on March 4, 1865. In his speech that day, the president spoke of being kind to the South after the war. Americans needed to work hard to "bind up the nation's wounds," he said.[3]

An OVERVIEW of the AMERICAN CIVIL WAR Through PRIMARY SOURCES

Southern cities now fell, one by one. The Union army took Petersburg, Virginia, on April 2. The following day, Richmond was captured. The war was over, and Lee knew it. "There is nothing left me but to go and see General Grant, and I would rather die a thousand deaths," he said.[4]

On April 9, Lee surrendered to Grant at Appomattox Court House, Virginia. The Southern soldiers could go home, taking their horses and mules with them. The men would need the animals to work their farms, Grant said.[5]

Can Davis Save the Confederacy?

Even after Lee's surrender, Jefferson Davis was trying to keep Confederate hopes alive. He had fled Richmond and was running the government from railroad cars in North Carolina. He hoped to find new soldiers who would keep fighting. But his officers told him the men were beaten and would not fight anymore. After the war, Davis was sent to prison for two years at Fortress Monroe, Virginia.

Peace at Last?

In this illustration, General Lee surrenders to General Grant at Appomattox Court House, Virginia.

There would be no more punishment. The country had suffered enough. After General Lee's surrender, a few final battles took place throughout the country. All fighting finally ended in May, with the surrender of the rest of the Confederate soldiers.

Five days after Lee surrendered, President Lincoln was shot while watching a play at Ford's Theatre in Washington, D.C. The killer was John Wilkes Booth, an actor from the South who believed in slavery and hated the president. Lincoln died the following day, April 15.

PRIMARY SOURCE

After the Civil War ended, the nation required much healing. Slavery had ended, but it would take many years of effort for African Americans to achieve equal rights. This battered and torn American flag was raised above Fort Sumter on April 14, 1865, four years after the first shots of the Civil War were fired.

Peace at Last?

As the nation mourned its president, it also faced a variety of other problems. The South had been left in ruins. Its cities and farmlands had been destroyed. One out of every five white Southern men had died in the war.

The Southern states needed to come back into the Union. But they had to get rid of their Confederate governments before they could be part of the United States.

The question of slavery was no longer a problem. But now what would happen to the 4 million freed black men and women? The nation needed to find a way to educate them, as well as to teach them job skills.

Not all Americans were willing to accept the former slaves as free citizens. For many years to come, black Americans would have to fight to be treated equally.

The Civil War was over; the Union was restored. But a new struggle was just beginning—the work of healing the nation.

TIMELINE

1619

August: First African slaves arrive in Jamestown, Virginia.

1793

Eli Whitney invents the cotton gin.

1860

November: Lincoln is elected president.
December: South Carolina is the first of eleven states to secede from the Union.

1861

February: Confederate States of America is formed.
April 12: Fort Sumter is attacked; the Civil War begins.
April 15: Lincoln calls for 75,000 army volunteers.
April 19: Lincoln orders a blockade of all Southern ports.
July 21: Confederacy wins the First Battle of Bull Run.

1862

February 6: Union captures Fort Henry.
February 16: Union captures Fort Donelson.
March: The Battle of the Ironclads takes place.
April 6–7: Union wins the Battle of Shiloh.
August 30: Confederacy wins the Second Battle of Bull Run.
September 17: Union claims victory at Battle of Antietam.
September 22: Lincoln issues a draft of the Emancipation Proclamation.
December 13: Confederacy wins Battle of Fredericksburg.

Timeline

1863

January 1: Lincoln issues the Emancipation Proclamation.
May: Confederacy wins at Chancellorsville, Virginia.
July 1–3: Union wins the Battle of Gettysburg.
July 4: Lee retreats from Gettysburg; Union takes Vicksburg.
July 11–13: New York City draft riots take place.
September: Confederate victory at Chickamauga, Georgia.

1864

May: Grant and Lee fight in the Wilderness.
July: Sherman begins his attack on Atlanta, Georgia.
September 2: Sherman takes Atlanta.
November: Lincoln is reelected; Sherman begins "March to the Sea."
December 21: Sherman captures Savannah, Georgia.

1865

February: Sherman takes Charleston, South Carolina.
March 4: Lincoln is sworn into office for his second term.
April 2: Union army captures Petersburg, Virginia.
April 3: Richmond is captured.
April 9: Lee surrenders at Appomattox Court House, Virginia, leading to the end of the Civil War.
April 15: Lincoln dies after being shot by John Wilkes Booth; Vice President Andrew Johnson becomes president.
December 6: The Thirteenth Amendment to the U.S. Constitution abolishes slavery everywhere in the United States.

CHAPTER NOTES

CHAPTER 1. NORTH AGAINST SOUTH

1. "If Slavery Is Not Wrong, Nothing Is Wrong," *Library of Congress,* n.d., <http://www.loc.gov/exhibits/treasures/trt027.html> (October 20, 2003).
2. "Jefferson Davis," *American Civil War.com,* n.d., <http://americancivilwar.com/south/jeffdavi.html> (October 20, 2003).
3. Geoffrey C. Ward, *The Civil War: An Illustrated History* (New York: Alfred A. Knopf, 1990), p. 30.
4. Shelby Foote, *The Civil War: Fort Sumter to Perryville* (New York: Random House, 1958), pp. 58–59.

CHAPTER 2. THE WAR BEGINS

1. Abraham Lincoln, *Speeches and Writings 1859–1865* (New York: The Library of America, 1989), p. 214.
2. Shelby Foote, *The Civil War: Fort Sumter to Perryville* (New York: Random House, 1958), p. 82.
3. Ibid., p. 80.

CHAPTER 3. MANY MORE BATTLES

1. University of Michigan, AFROTC Detachment 390, <http://www.umich.edu/~det390/cadets/cwing/wing/hambey.html> (October 20, 2003).
2. Shelby Foote, *The Civil War: Fort Sumter to Perryville* (New York: Random House, 1958), p. 212.
3. Geoffrey C. Ward, *The Civil War: An Illustrated History* (New York: Alfred A. Knopf, 1990), p. 114.
4. Robert E. Denney, *The Civil War Years: A Day-by-Day Chronicle* (New York: Gramercy Books, 1992), p. 152.
5. Ward, p. 281.
6. Abraham Lincoln, *Speeches and Writings 1859–1865* (New York: The Library of America, 1989), p. 323.
7. Shelby Foote, *The Civil War: Fort Sumter to Perryville* (New York: Random House, 1958), p. 702.

Chapter Notes

8. Stephen B. Oates, *With Malice Toward None: The Life of Abraham Lincoln* (New York: Harper & Row, 1977), p. 309.
9. "The Emancipation Proclamation," *National Park Service*, n.d., <http://www.nps.gov/ncro/anti/emancipation.html> (October 20, 2003).

CHAPTER 4. THE TIDE TURNS

1. Champ Clark, *Gettysburg: The Confederate High Tide* (Alexandria, Va.: Time-Life Books, 1985), p. 143.
2. Bell Irvin Wiley, *The Life of Johnny Reb* (Baton Rouge, La.: Louisiana State University Press, 1978), p. 93.
3. Bruce Catton, *Gettysburg: The Final Fury* (Garden City, N.Y.: Doubleday & Co., Inc., 1974), p. 93.
4. James M. Merrill, *William Tecumseh Sherman* (New York: Rand McNally & Company, 1971), p. 238.
5. Robert E. Denney, *The Civil War Years: A Day-by-Day Chronicle* (New York: Gramercy Books, 1992), p. 453.

CHAPTER 5. PEACE AT LAST?

1. Geoffrey C. Ward, *The Civil War: An Illustrated History* (New York: Alfred A. Knopf, 1990), p. 344.
2. Editors of Time-Life Books, *War Between Brothers* (Alexandria, Virginia: Time-Life Books, 1996), p. 176.
3. Abraham Lincoln, "Second Inaugural Address," *Bartleby.com*, 2012, <http://www.bartleby.com/124/pres32.html> (October 20, 2003).
4. Emory M. Thomas, *Robert E. Lee: A Biography* (New York: W. W. Norton, 1995), p. 362.
5. Bruce Catton, *U.S. Grant and the American Military Tradition* (New York: Grosset & Dunlap, 1954), p. 128.

GLOSSARY

blockade—Closing off a city or harbor so no one can get in or out.

Confederate States of America (or Confederacy)—The separate country formed by eleven southern states that left the United States: Alabama, Arkansas, Florida, Georgia, Louisiana, Mississippi, North Carolina, South Carolina, Tennessee, Texas, and Virginia.

Emancipation Proclamation—Lincoln's document that freed the slaves in the rebelling Southern states.

ironclad—A ship with iron on the outside. In the Civil War, they were made of wood and coated with iron above the deck.

secede—To break away from.

terms of surrender—Conditions that generals agree to at surrender, such as giving up weapons or prison for the losing troops.

territory—An area of the country that is not a state but has its own lawmakers.

U.S. Constitution—A paper describing the government's powers and the rights of the American people. It contains the basic laws of the United States.

FURTHER READING

Books

Hiller, Sandra J. *Turning Point Battles of the Civil War.* New York: Crabtree Publishing, 2011.

Murphy, Jim. *A Savage Thunder: Antietam and the Bloody Road to Freedom.* New York: Margaret K. McElderry Books, 2009.

Nemeth, Jason D. *Voices of the Civil War: Stories From the Battlefields.* Mankato, Minn.: Capstone Press, 2011.

Weber, Jennifer L. *Summer's Bloodiest Days: The Battle of Gettysburg as Told From All Sides.* Washington, D.C.: National Geographic, 2010.

Internet Addresses

Library of Congress: Timeline of the Civil War
<http://memory.loc.gov/ammem/cwphtml/tl1861.html>

PBS: The Civil War
<http://www.pbs.org/civilwar/>

INDEX

A
Anderson, Robert, 14, 37,
Appomattox Court House, 38
Atlanta, Georgia, 35, 36

B
Barber, Luke, 25
battles
    Antietam, 26, 27
    Ball's Bluff, 20
    Bull Run, 16–17, 19, 20
    Bull Run, second, 26–27
    Chancellorsville, 30
    Fort Henry, 21
    Fort Donelson, 21
    Fort Sumter, 13–14, 16, 37
    Gettysburg, 31–33, 34
    Manassas, 16, 19
    Seven Days', 26
    Shiloh Church, 22, 25
    Wilderness, 34
Beauregard, Pierre, 16
"Bleeding Kansas," 9
blockade, 15–16
Booth, John Wilkes, 39
Buell, Don Carlos, 22, 25
Burnside, Ambrose, 29

C
Confederacy (Confederate States of America), 11
    advantages, 15
    army, 16, 26, 27, 30
    secession, 9, 10, 11, 26
    surrender to Union, 38–39
cotton gin, 8

D
Davis, Jefferson, 11, 14, 38
drafting soldiers, 33

E
Emancipation Proclamation, 28

F
15th Illinois Regiment, 25
Ford's Theatre, 39

G
Grant, Ulysses S., 21, 22–23, 25, 33, 34, 38

H
Hooker, Joseph, 29–30, 31

J
Jackson, Thomas J. "Stonewall," 19, 30
Jefferson, Thomas, 6
Johnston, Albert S., 22, 23

L
Lee, Robert E., 26, 27, 29, 30–32, 34, 38–39
Lincoln, Abraham, 9, 13, 36, 37
    death, 39
    military decisions, 14–15, 19, 20, 25, 27, 31, 33
    and slavery, 9, 27–28, 29
    speeches, 37

M
Madison, James, 6
McClellan, George B., 20–21, 25–26, 27
McDowell, Irvin, 16
Meade, George, 31
Merrimack, 23
Monitor, 23

P
Pickett, George, 34
Pickett's Charge, 34

R
rebel yell, 19

S
Sherman, William Tecumseh, 11, 33, 35
    march to the sea, 36
slavery, 4, 5–7, 8–9, 11, 26, 27–28, 39, 40, 41
Stuart, James E. B. "Jeb," 30

U
uniforms, 17
Union
    advantages, 15
    army, 16, 20, 21, 25, 29, 31, 34, 38
    cavalry, 31
    navy, 15–16, 21
U.S. Constitution, 6–7

W
West Point, 21, 26
Whitney, Eli, 8